THE GROWTH JOURNEY

THE GROWTH JOURNEY

MARLOWE SINCLAIR

CONTENTS

Introduction

Success isn't a one-size-fits-all journey, and this book dives deep into navigating the paths that lead to both personal and professional triumph. Aimed at young professionals, college and university students, career seekers, and business leaders, it addresses the key aspects of growth in an ever-evolving economic landscape. This guidance is designed to help you become an invaluable team member, adapt to workplace changes, and if you're already an entrepreneur, find the critical ingredients for successful business ventures.

The foundational principles introduced in this chapter will be expanded upon in the subsequent sections. These aren't mere philosophical musings; they're transformative insights that have impacted lives, careers, and enterprises. Whether you're a novice or a seasoned professional, the concepts outlined here will offer valuable perspectives and practical tools. Each chapter will begin with the genesis of an idea and its tested perspectives, followed by practical applications and concluding with thought-provoking questions to challenge your understanding and spur growth.

Purpose and Scope of the Book

In today's fast-paced world, personal and career growth is more accessible than ever. This book is designed to help readers identify crucial areas of employability, gain comprehensive knowledge, and continuously assess and enhance their worth. By uncovering latent skills and actively pursuing employment opportunities in these areas, readers can significantly elevate their professional prospects.

The book's content spans an extensive range of knowledge, catering to employers' demand for individuals with holistic growth. This is not just another self-help book; it's a strategic guide to navigating the critical aspects of modern employment. From crafting compelling CVs to mastering emotional intelligence and understanding organizational dynamics, this book addresses twelve essential themes crucial to career success.

Unlike typical self-development publications, this book offers unique insights into how companies evaluate potential employees and leverage their skills. The proprietary Content Index covers advanced topics rarely found in conventional literature, providing readers with a comprehensive understanding of the hiring process from a microeconomic perspective. This invaluable resource is a one-stop guide for mastering the art of employability and achieving unparalleled personal and professional growth.

Chapter 1: Understanding Personal Growth

Learning chess and honing your talents isn't so different from personal growth—you need to nurture your natural abilities to avoid squandering them. Think of personal development as a roadmap with strategies to guide you. Here, it's about mastering cognitive intelligence, embracing unique personality traits, and adapting to your environment.

Growth is about evolving for the better. It's not just for intellectuals but for anyone: entrepreneurs, technopreneurs, teachers, students, even church workers. Whether consciously or not, personal growth is achieved through hard work, self-signing, and coaching. This book emphasizes that true value lies in aligning with the pillars of life, not just theoretical concepts. Let's tackle these key questions head-on.

What is Personal Growth?

Personal growth encompasses self-empowerment principles, life coaching, skills development, and credentials. It's a mix of motivation, creativity, responsibility, potential, vision, goals, confidence, productivity, lifestyle, relationships, and more. It's the antithesis of dependency, victimization, procrastination, and a slew of other negative traits.

Growing personally is a comprehensive study, a deliberate decision, a firm commitment, and an enriching journey. It involves removing excess thinking and building constructive, respectful agreements with others. Personal growth is like taming a wild horse—you need to learn to think, step, act, and enjoy together.

Why Personal Growth Matters

Growth is essential for success in any area of life—spiritually, physically, professionally. Look around, and you'll see that everyone who's successful has grown to get there. Life is dynamic; you either move forward or fall behind. There are no seat belts on the road to growth—no time to slow down.

When you grow personally, you enhance your career effectiveness, contribute more to your organizations, and improve various life aspects, including relationships. Growth can be an engine driving us to success or a brake holding us back. The best strategy? Grow a little every day.

Chapter 2: Setting Goals and Vision

Setting Goals and Vision

To truly thrive in personal and career growth, setting goals and envisioning success are indispensable. Goals act like a guiding star, shaping our choices and priorities and making our journey practical. Envisioning is about having a vivid picture of a future, filled with sensory representations and emotional resonance, which helps in articulating valuable outcomes that we strongly believe in.

Setting goals coupled with a vision gives us a competitive edge. Goals bridge the gap between a focused vision and the achievement of outcomes, fueled by a strong desire and belief in our abilities. Many organizations articulate their mission through well-crafted statements, but for individuals, building a vision translates into clearly defined future indicators. This approach can apply to all life aspects, where greatness is achieved by having specific, targeted goals.

The Importance of Goals

Goal-setting is a fundamental message echoed in personal mastery workshops: those who set and pursue goals consciously and consistently achieve higher performance. Goals are the seeds of success, mental concepts that steer individuals toward positive actions leading to desired results. Successful people create plans, use positive self-talk, reaffirm their goals, and identify crucial activities that propel them toward their desired outcomes.

For instance, setting simple targets helped me run and complete two marathons. Clear goals about the training schedule kept me motivated, outlining the physical activities required to meet the race's demands. This structured approach illustrates how setting and affirming goals foster commitment and accomplishment, be it in running or any career endeavor.

Creating a Vision for Success

Achieving anything significant begins with envisioning the end goal. Our thoughts precede actions, making the creation of a success vision the first step in pursuing personal or career goals. A comprehensive vision reflects our dreams, values, and needs, charting a high-level course to attain goals with a clear blueprint of strategies and desired outcomes.

Visualizing successful outcomes enhances motivation and commitment, making goals feel personal and emotional. This "dream" stage transforms goal-setting into an emotional and practical intersection, fueling productivity and driving commitment. When goals align with personal values and evoke deep feelings, they are more likely to be achieved.

Chapter 3: Self-Awareness and Reflection

Self-Awareness and Reflection

Being mindful of who you are now and over time is key to personal and career growth. Just as a company tests a new product, you can conduct "self-testing" through reflection. This involves assessing what works, what doesn't, and what you need to develop for your future self. Reflecting on experiences is crucial for developing insights and new understandings.

Self-awareness and reflection are also essential for a spiritual journey, which includes exploring self-identity and purpose. Gaining deep insights can help you handle complex situations effectively and develop a new worldview with significant personal, organizational, and community impacts.

The Power of Self-Awareness

Knowing your limits enhances your strengths, at least in the eyes of others. Self-awareness doesn't eliminate the need for improvement but helps focus your strategies. It forms the foundation of emotional intelligence, distinguishing between being skilled and wise in relationships. Those who know themselves can confidently adjust their behaviors, thoughts, and communications to leverage strengths and minimize weaknesses.

Understanding what's important for your success and the barriers you face begins with self-awareness. Each career coaching session aims to help individuals answer these questions and grow in self-belief, recognizing that career progress is limited only by imagination and determination. Feedback on these topics will shape future career development.

Practicing Reflection

"Socrates said the unexamined life is not worth living." Reflecting on life helps us learn from experiences and plan for the future. Mezirow notes that we are products of our perspectives formed during reflection. This understanding helps you realize you're more than your past experiences.

Reflection enables gaining insights into learning, seeing where you've come from, where you are, and mapping out strategies for the future. Blüher highlights how reflection develops practical wisdom and moral consciousness, improving decision-making. It helps balance priorities without overwhelming yourself, emphasizing the value of work-life balance and creating well-rounded, confident individuals.

Chapter 4: Building Resilience

The Importance of Resilience

The central theme of this chapter is resilience—the capacity to recover quickly from difficulties and face adversities with strength and flexibility. On the surface, resilience is the ability to handle whatever life throws at you. It's about bouncing back, staying strong in challenging situations, and responding effectively in the moment. Resilient people are less likely to break under pressure, burn out, become demotivated, or fall prey to emotional turmoil.

The good news is that resilience isn't a fixed trait but can be cultivated, grown, and developed over time with practice, patience, endurance, and struggle. Whether it's winning a tough race, climbing a rock face, or even beating a video game, the thrill lies in overcoming obstacles, growing in the process, and gaining the necessary strength and competence for optimal success.

While resilience can set the stage for victory, restore confidence, and ensure persistence, it plays an even more critical role in achieving success. In short, resilience fuels progress. Everyone faces rejection, setbacks, obstacles, and failure at some point. Acting as a protective factor, resilience decreases the psychological and medical risks of breaking under pressure, enabling you to perform at your best, even in the face of significant challenges. When adversity strikes, it is resilience that will get you through it.

Understanding Resilience

Resilience is the ability to adapt to and overcome obstacles, bounce back from significant stresses, and move beyond adverse experiences. It can be seen as personal toughness. To fully grasp resilience, we need to explore related concepts and acknowledge its importance in personal and career contexts.

Resilience is a vital personal resource that helps individuals respond to and recover from setbacks. It involves employing aware, thoughtful, and judgmental thinking to navigate difficult or unexpected situations. In careers, resilience is crucial because everyone faces various challenges—being passed over for a promotion, termination, harassment, being left out, laid off, or burned out. Each of these difficulties requires different forms of resilience. For example, being laid off might be less psychologically damaging if you have strong personal resilience, even though both scenarios involve job loss.

Resilience doesn't eliminate difficulties or replace poor career conditions, but it equips you with the ability to solve problems and grow from tough situations. Awareness of your own resilience can also enhance it further.

Strategies for Building Resilience

Building resilience involves a variety of strategies that can be applied to different aspects of life. Some key strategies include:

1. **Cultivating Social Support:** Building a strong network of friends and family can provide emotional support during tough times.

2. **Backup Plans:** Having contingency plans, like backup child care, can help manage stress when life's priorities conflict.
3. **Physical Health:** Practicing good physical health through exercise, a balanced diet, and sufficient sleep strengthens your ability to cope with stress.

Resilience means continuing despite adversity, finding ways to move forward instead of being knocked out by negative events. Effective resilience strategies can be applied across various life areas to embrace crises and bring out the best in yourself. These strategies include:

- **Cognitive Appraisal:** Training your mind to assess situations positively.
- **Problem-Focused Coping:** Developing strategies to solve problems directly.
- **Rational Goal-Setting:** Setting realistic recovery objectives.
- **Social Connectedness:** Relying more on informal supports like family.
- **Optimism and Humor:** Maintaining a positive outlook and a good sense of humor.
- **Proactive Coping:** Preparing in advance for potential stressors.
- **Balanced Lifestyle:** Encouraging improved physical health through regular exercise, a nutritious diet, and proper sleep.

Coping literature highlights the importance of emotional expression and avoiding avoidant coping styles. For example, work-life conflict is a common issue people face, juggling numerous commitments and personal success markers. Recognizing and addressing these conflicts can help build resilience and identity.

Chapter 5: Developing Emotional Intelligence

The Role of Emotional Intelligence

Emotional intelligence (EQ) is a cornerstone of personal and career success, influencing your ability to balance emotions in various life aspects—business, relationships, and personal life. Developing EQ involves understanding and managing your own emotions and recognizing and responding to others' emotions.

Have you felt uplifted after helping someone or relieved after sharing your troubles with a friend? These instances highlight emotional intelligence—understanding and managing your emotions and interpreting others' emotions. Further areas to develop include managing relationships, making informed decisions, handling stress, feedback, and change. These aspects require high emotional intelligence for effective outcomes and the energy to navigate emerging work-life distractions. EQ is intrinsic to anyone seeking repeated success in life, driving your belief in handling new demands.

What is Emotional Intelligence?

Emotional intelligence, introduced by psychologists John Mayer and Peter Salovey in 1990, involves perceiving, managing, and evaluating emotions productively. EQ is crucial as emotions drive most decisions, affecting work performance, relationships, and mental well-being. Emotional intelligence encompasses several psychological strands, such as affect theory and cognitive psychology, and includes emotional literacy, regulation, and efficacy.

- **Emotional Literacy:** Awareness of emotions in oneself and others, and the ability to identify them.
- **Emotional Regulation:** Managing emotions appropriately.
- **Emotional Self-Efficacy:** Belief in one's ability to perform emotional tasks.
- **Understanding Emotions:** Knowing the causes and predicting emotional reactions.

Developing EQ is complex, requiring understanding emotions' roots and their implications in various situations. It's a vital asset for personal and career development, helping people better understand themselves and others.

Enhancing Emotional Intelligence Skills

Improving EQ skills is the focus here, with seven key guidelines and focus areas detailed. These guidelines help managers and employees enhance emotional awareness and apply strategies to develop emotional abilities through stories, exercises, or journaling projects, embracing an experiential and practical focus.

The intervention targets personal and professional improvements, such as bettering relationships and enhancing communication and decision-making skills. It educates about potential communication issues at different emotional skill levels and encourages reflection on approaches and strategies used.

Assuming emotions affect all life areas, exercises start with emotional self-awareness, linking to personal experiences and building on learned skills. Understanding how emotions impact interpersonal relationships is another focus, with scenarios and journaling integral to the intervention.

A list of good listeners' characteristics and benefits follows, encouraging students to infer these traits through assignments. The "open-ended" nature means previous assignments contribute to this one, allowing students to demonstrate their developed skills in identifying good listeners' characteristics. Softening questions and emphasizing journaling's private nature are key to successful exercises.

CHAPTER 7

Chapter 6: Effective Communication

The Importance of Communication Skills

Improving communication skills is crucial for personal growth and career success. Effective communication helps build better relationships with family, colleagues, and others, making it easier to reach your goals. How you communicate impacts the quality of your relationships and your ability to connect with people around you.

Forming close interpersonal relationships relies heavily on communication skills. The way we communicate can influence the performance of those around us, affect leadership acceptance, and shape ideas. Effective communication can prevent or resolve many conflicts. People make decisions based on how they relate and understand one another, and the quality of life is closely tied to communication abilities. Those who communicate their feelings well tend to succeed and be understood by others. Effective communication is vital for leadership, allowing ideas to be shared and fostering productive collaborations.

The Role of Communication in Success

Success hinges on effective communication—getting your message across clearly. While everyone can succeed, not everyone gets the chance. Successful people often have the right kind of confidence, largely due to their communication skills. Enduring success is rooted in the ability to create and sustain interest in others, be it prospects or customers.

Mass communication, such as advertising, also relies on effective communication. Success isn't just about what you say, but how you say it. In a competitive society, communication is key to growth. Pay close attention to how you communicate, as it can shape your life's course. All great stories have strong structures, and the same goes for a successful career. Understanding and implementing a solid communication structure is crucial.

Improving Communication Skills

"The Growth Journey" covers practical tips and tools for improving communication skills and building rapport. These strategies can enhance performance and improve the bottom line.

Open communication with employees is vital. Discuss why employees may not communicate openly and explore strategies to address this. An employee share program, results interrogation, and performance appraisals are part of fostering open communication. Addressing workplace stress can reduce expensive staff turnover and improve overall effectiveness.

Good communication skills involve effectively conveying ideas, knowledge, plans, and goals. These skills improve performance and minimize stress. Effective time management, linked to communication, boosts performance and productivity, enhancing personal and professional careers. Reducing stress and improving time management also increase personal confidence.

CHAPTER 8

Chapter 7: Time Management and Productivity

The Importance of Time Management

Imagine starting your day knowing exactly where your time will be most effective. A manager at Federated Insurance Companies once organized a meeting where each manager drew an outline of Minnesota. The lesson? Without a clear goal (knowing what Minnesota looks like), even our best efforts can fall short. We can only map out an effective growth journey when we truly understand our goals and prioritize our time accordingly.

Starting your day with activities aligned with your major goals significantly boosts your productivity. If our performance at work is to be optimal, we must first identify the key achievements and accomplishments required. In sales, time management breaks down into four core areas: planning, prioritizing, executing, and evaluating.

The Importance of Time Management

Time management often transforms initial skepticism into realization. Many introverted clients were hesitant at first but saw significant change once they began to manage their time effectively.

Effective time management directly impacts your vocational commitments and relationships.

By applying these strategies, you will enhance your ability to allocate time and resources effectively, leading to greater trust and efficiency. Successful time management focuses on using your time wisely, ensuring that your efforts align with your goals and commitments.

Strategies for Enhancing Productivity

Now that you have an overview of the Growth Journey, let's explore specific strategies to enhance productivity. These strategies are crucial whether you work for an employer or yourself, as they help you produce better and more significant results.

1. **Energy Management:** Focus on managing your energy rather than your time. Alternate between periods of intense work and well-planned rest to avoid burnout.
2. **Workflow Management:** Develop a systematic way of categorizing tasks and commit to completing them as part of a daily ritual.
3. **Pareto Principle:** Prioritize tasks that yield the most significant results. Focus on the vital few rather than the trivial many.
4. **Batching:** Group similar tasks together to reduce inefficiencies. While this strategy improves focus, be mindful of monotony and ensure tasks remain engaging.

By integrating these strategies into your routine, you can significantly boost your productivity and effectiveness, paving the way for personal and professional growth.

Chapter 8: Continuous Learning and Growth

The Importance of Continuous Learning

Influencing a team or community to grow is immensely rewarding. Since 1995, my work mentoring university students has been incredibly fulfilling. Watching a student grow in knowledge and confidence, learn to critically reflect, and embrace feedback is a joy. It significantly impacts their lives, enhancing the team's knowledge base, building morale, and fostering motivation. These conversations about personal journeys and careers contribute to creating a 'talent pipeline' and fostering a 'learning culture'.

A wise woman once told me, "If you stop learning, you start dying." While dramatic, it underscores that learning is essential for effectiveness and career success. In some countries, like the US, 15% of a manager's training occurs within their organization, while the remaining 85% is 'self-directed learning'. On average, middle managers engage in 140 hours of development annually. This continuous learning is essential for providing valuable advice and maintaining a broad general business acumen alongside deep technical expertise. It's an ongoing journey, not a one-time event.

The Value of Lifelong Learning

Lifelong learning prepares you for the entirety of your career, not just its beginning. Educational systems aim to equip you with the skills necessary for getting a job, but lifelong learning is designed for continuous personal and professional growth. In a recent survey, two-thirds of respondents viewed education's primary goal as job preparation. This preparation, focused on lifelong learning, is essential for career advancement.

The economic benefits of lifelong learning are significant. It strengthens your skills for current roles and prepares you for future opportunities. Personal goal progress improves life satisfaction, as seen with companies like Dow Chemical and 3M. Continuous learning also enhances productivity, even through leisure activities like photography or music. The popularity of programs like U3A and TAFE among retirees demonstrates the widespread value of lifelong learning.

Methods for Continuous Growth

Ensuring continuous growth in personal and career life involves methods that promote constant development. These methods create a conducive learning environment for day-to-day activities.

Personally, embrace new ways of thinking by asking yourself questions that awaken a desire to learn more and incorporate new methods. In your career, it's easy to get stuck and stop growing if you become too comfortable. Follow guidelines that foster growth, adapt to changing environments, and develop soft skills like learning agility, critical observation, local systems awareness, self-awareness, and self-regard.

Embrace methods of continuous growth to ensure you are always advancing toward your goals, adapting not just for change's sake but for meaningful development.

Chapter 9: Building a Support Network

Why it's Important
Having the right mindset and engaging the help of others during times of challenge and growth makes us stronger. We all need someone to encourage us, suggest new options when we feel boxed in, and challenge us when we make excuses. These people help us stay resilient and move forward despite setbacks. Our network can be our cheering section, information center, introduction committee, naysayer alert council, and devil's advocate.

For career advancement, a strong network provides insider information about organizations, industries, and trends. Networks offer new ways to raise capital, enhance market penetration, and increase sales. They give access to mentors who offer unvarnished insights into our blind spots and strengths. Our network is a place to explore "what if..." questions for careers and opportunities. If unsure what to do next, start by growing your network. Personal growth and building a support network are anchored in the time spent developing and nurturing relationships with partners, family, and close friends who help us grow.

The Importance of a Support System

Hard work and commitment alone aren't enough for success. We weren't prepared for the loss, failure, and fears that come with achieving our goals. Competition is stiffer, and rewards seem distant. Fear doesn't stop ambition, but a support system provides the will and strength to keep trying.

Many struggle to find themselves, their career path, or new relationships without a support system. Downsizing becomes torturous without camaraderie and fellowship. Living in isolation makes achievements feel unrecognized. Family should provide a steady shoulder, reassurance, and unconditional empathy. Societies must recognize the importance of support systems for sustainable success.

Strategies for Establishing a Support Network

- **Join Local Associations:** Meet successful people in your field who can connect you to mentors and encourage your growth.
- **Volunteer Work:** Build networking relationships through collaborative work.
- **Reassess Current Relationships:** Spend time with people who attract the best in others and share a positive attitude.
- **Engage in New Hobbies:** Meet new people in classes or social groups outside your current circle.
- **Diversify Your Network:** Surround yourself with people of diverse talents and experiences committed to making a difference.
- **Online Networking:** Join professional groups or forums, and engage on networking sites like LinkedIn.

When networking, focus on getting to know the other person. Even in a brief conversation, ask questions and listen. For finding a mentor, make appointments to meet industry professionals. Aim to leave meetings with new contacts and a better understanding of the field. Follow up with a "Thank You Note" and continue the cycle.

Chapter 10: Overcoming Challenges and Obstacles

The Growth Journey

Embarking on the growth journey is a lifelong adventure of self-discovery. It's not a straightforward path, as life's inevitable obstacles will test our resolve. While initial progress might seem smooth, adversity and struggle are guaranteed. Finding the fortitude to continue despite challenges is crucial. Without understanding resilience, the growth journey becomes a tough ride.

Beyond resilience, we need mental tools for rapid and effective problem-solving to navigate the myriad obstacles. We may face battles such as low self-esteem, procrastination, depression, job loss, and more. How we handle these adversities will determine our success in our careers.

Common Challenges to Growth

The growth journey includes various stages, each with potential challenges. The 12 Step Model outlines how development unfolds and the opportunities it provides for change, learning, and innovation. However, each step can present serious challenges. Recognizing these challenges and understanding how they impede growth is vital.

Common challenges include getting stuck at a certain step, difficulty progressing, or resisting change. These obstacles often stem from a lack of awareness of inner resources. By reviewing these challenges, individuals can better prepare for growth interventions and appreciate the potential growth at each step.

Effective Problem-Solving Strategies

Problem-solving can invigorate coping mechanisms and stimulate satisfaction within a group. It involves a series of decisions, typically following eight key steps under two general duties: defining problems and decision-making.

A structured approach to problem-solving increases the likelihood of quick and successful solutions. Effectively using this model helps progress ideas step-by-step and signals when a problem is resolved. Implementing such strategies ensures continuous growth and the ability to overcome challenges.

Chapter 11: Celebrating Success and Milestones

The Importance of Celebrating Success

Acknowledging individual and corporate triumphs doubles their value and meaning. Celebrating success announces to your mind, "Hey, you're okay, and this is what I wanted to achieve!" Often, we shy away from the spotlight due to self-esteem issues. But taking a moment to celebrate boosts self-worth and confidence.

When you lose a job, face a breakup, or encounter personal setbacks, a positive mindset can help you see new opportunities. Celebrating successes, big or small, is essential. In the corporate world, celebrating a sales increase, for instance, recognizes collective effort and boosts morale. Celebrations needn't be extravagant; small, meaningful acknowledgments are just as impactful.

The Importance of Acknowledging Achievements

In the Growth LifeWheels course, we ask students to write down recent achievements. Initially, many struggle, but upon reflection, they recognize numerous accomplishments. Often, we believe we must achieve grand things to relax and celebrate.

Celebrating achievements fosters gratitude, appreciation, and acknowledgment of your efforts. It supports growth and creates feelings of contentment, joy, and happiness. Developing a mindset of acknowledgment, even for small achievements, can break down barriers to personal and professional development.

Ways to Celebrate Success

Celebrating success doesn't always require grand events. Here are some ways to recognize and enjoy your achievements:

- **Reward Yourself:** Splurge on a gift or treat yourself to something nice.
- **Go on Vacation:** Take time off to appreciate your victory and let go of past struggles.
- **Throw a Party:** Spend quality time with friends, share a meal, and enjoy each other's company.
- **Do What Makes You Happy:** Engage in activities that bring you joy and motivate future accomplishments.
- **Relish the Journey:** Keep track of favorite moments and share them with friends and family.
- **Pump Yourself Up:** Celebrate with fun activities to maintain positive energy.
- **Look Forward to the Next Victory:** Embrace each moment and set new goals.
- **Create a Celebration Ritual:** Mark your achievements with special activities that create lasting memories.

CHAPTER 13

Chapter 12: Sustaining Growth and Momentum

The Real Imperative

Although this book focuses on "Growth," sustaining the achieved growth is the true imperative. Having addressed different aspects—individual, team, and organization—the final part discusses strategies and processes for lasting achievements. Before delving into these, recognize the satisfaction from the effort and determination put into making significant changes. Sustaining growth and momentum is an ongoing journey, never fully mastered. Progress relies on small, consistent steps that accumulate into great strides. When sustaining improvements, the success lies in the accumulation of numerous small actions done correctly.

The concept of three burners—depicting individual change capability—is crucial. These burners, representing different levels, must be maintained with a high flame of change. They are interconnected and vital for sustaining growth in ourselves, our teams, and functional areas. At the macro level, these burners relate to organizational change capability and the ability to drive sustainable change.

Maintaining Consistency in Growth Efforts

Consistency in growth efforts is essential for maintaining a positive approach and ensuring continuous improvement. Consistent effort invariably leads to breakthroughs, though the time required may vary. To maintain consistency, consider:

- **Listening to Podcasts:** Explore strategies to improve in areas of interest.
- **Reading Good Books:** Apply the knowledge gained from insightful reading.
- **Seeking Mentorship:** Find a superior who can mentor and guide you.

Understanding which skills are valuable and usable is crucial for continued growth. Good habits, followed consistently, become assets. Prioritizing, building relationships, and envisioning future goals are examples of successful growth strategies. The assets discussed here are not exhaustive, but they provide a foundation for sustained growth.

Strategies for Long-Term Success

Long-term success requires openness to change, questioning and reconsidering beliefs, and altering actions where necessary. Confirm what works, reinforce successful strategies, and discard what doesn't. Living in "the moment" with proper planning and preparation supports decisive execution.

Reinforcing your position involves honoring products, services, self-worth, and the uniqueness of each customer and colleague. Great visionaries change the hearts of social or business enterprises, while effective managers execute business objectives efficiently. Long-term strategies connect personal and career growth with broader strategic company plans, promoting an autonomous and responsible work ethic.

From now on, you are responsible for mapping out your personal and career growth strategies. Here are a few suggestions to guide you:

- Reflect on achievements and set new goals.
- Regularly update your skills and knowledge.
- Foster a growth mindset and remain adaptable.

CHAPTER 14

Conclusion

We have reached the end of our growth journey, having asked and answered 12 critical questions designed to push your thinking and generate deep insights. The work in Personal Mastery, Leadership Development, and High-Performance Organizational Development complements this journey. We need excellent tools, robust processes, and profound knowledge of self to manage our internal growth for personal and career success. Without integrating organizational reflections on individual journeys, we risk self-sabotage and disappointment. Here are some core questions to ponder:

1. How have my personal circumstances shaped my current life?
2. What were the critical times of change when I felt the most growth?
3. What contributions have increased my inner security and confidence?
4. What unique contributions do I bring to my organization in terms of talent, skills, and networks?
5. What failures could be springboards for greater success?
6. How have I planned my next career move, and what are my success measures?
7. What makes my career unique, and is it right for me?

8. What evidence shows I am rebuilding and reinventing my career?
9. What is my career plan for the next 10 years?
10. What evidence shows I have been successful, and how will the organization notice?

Key Takeaways

This book avoids offering ten simple steps to success. Instead, it asks critical questions, subjected to three 'relevancy' filters:

1. Does it make sense? Is it used personally, in the company, and advised to friends and family?
2. Is it simple and practical?
3. Does it demonstrate expertise and intelligence, or does it 'free the captive' as GSM often advocates?

Even one implementable idea can save months or years of stagnation. Use a utility approach to make every idea work for you. Highlight and jot reminders as you relate case studies to your growth. Use this process to reconsider, redefine, and reassert your personal and career growth objectives. These case studies often address critical questions surrounding growth.

CHAPTER 15

Appendix: Additional Resources

We wanted to offer you additional resources referenced in our session. Grow With Us. If this book has piqued your curiosity, consider joining one of our personal or professional development programs. Visit the Programs tab on our website to learn more and get started on your growth journey.

Other Resources and Books

- **Built to Last: Successful Habits of Visionary Companies** by Jim Collins & Jerry Porras
- **Flower Exercise: Discover your Core Purpose**
- **Love, Service, Freedom** offering from Business Resource Lab, Berkana Institute, 4100-20 St. Suite #220, San Francisco, CA 94114
- **Values Driven Change in Alberta's Nonprofits** developed by volunteer Naming-Pinal groups working with the Volunteer and Information Centre Edmonton
- **Before You Think Another Thought: An Illustrated Guide to Exponential Wisdom** by Bruce I. Doyle III by Aigauge Systems 2004

- **Quantify Your Happiness** Prime Solutions, Inc. 6919 Out-ingdale Road Somerset, California 95684 U.S.A.

Other Key Topics

- **The Success Principles** by Jack Canfield
- **Falling Upward** by Richard Rohr
- **The Anatomy of Peace: Resolving the Heart of Conflict** by The Arbinger Institute
- **Deep Change: Discovering the Leader Within** by Robert E. Quinn
- **Focas: Finding My Way Back to Me** by Summer Donily
- **Getting to Yes: Negotiating Agreement Without Giving In** by Roger Fisher and William Ury

As we grew, we discovered several additional resources that are now part of our program offerings. Read more about them and sign up on our website under the Programs tab.

Ready to dive in and continue your growth journey? Let's make it happen!

www.ingramcontent.com/pod-product-compliance
Lightning Source LLC
Chambersburg PA
CBHW031134160726
47989CB00017B/2970